MY LIFE'S POETRY

I0098982

Volume 1

Author: Lalea M.M. King

* First Printing in the United States of America 2015 *

Imprint: Lalea's Inspirational Poetry

Publication of: Irish Writing & Publishing (IWP)

Some passages in this book have been paraphrased from the King James Version Bible.

ISBN 9780692611524

CONTENTS

DEDICATIONS

This book is dedicated to all those, whether male or female, who have survived abuse.

Whether the abuse was sexual, physical, mental, or emotional, I hope that these words give you hope and direction to let you know that Christ does love you and wants to heal you.

You survived what you went through to be a beacon of light for someone else.

Do not let anger and bitterness reside within you any longer. The best revenge you can have is to forgive your abuser and allow God to love you and to teach you how to love yourself, others, and especially the one (s) who caused you hurt.

"For the weapons of our warfare are not carnal but mighty through God to the pulling down of strongholds." KJV II Corinthians 10:4

If you are reading these words, you are already an over-comer. You still have life, which means you still have *hope*!

ACKNOWLEDGMENTS

First and foremost, I would like to give thanks to Christ who has brought me through every trial and has watched over me. My faith has carried me through so much in this life. Thank you for teaching me through your Holy Spirit that things happen in this life due to a fallen world and not because you don't love me. It was your love that didn't allow me to be destroyed. It was your love that healed me and continues to heal me from the actions of others and even my own bad actions that has caused hurt in my life. It is your love that has opened the door and taught me how to recognize, receive and give real love from the heart. I give you all the glory allowing my life story to be an encouragement to myself and others, to allow my hurt to become a source of healing and to bless me with such a wonderful gift of exhortation which gives me purpose.

I want to thank my husband Shawn I. Stroud for supporting me in the publishing of this book. You came into my life when I was not only ready but also trying to give up. In a short amount of time God gave you a heart for me that reminded me that I am somebody. Through you, He reminded me that I do make a difference and that I can love. I love you so much and thank God for you. You have loved me through so much in such a short period of time and I pray that we have many more years together.

I want to thank Irish Jordan-Armstrong for believing in me. You came into my life at time when I prayed for Godly connections. It is because of you, this book, which was in me since 2003, has now been brought into fruition. You are a beautiful soul and have an awesome gift to help people to share their story with the world. I believe God for many souls to be healed and delivered because of your obedience. Thank you for your patience and loving spirit.

Janet (King) Perry, my grandmother who raised me and watched over me most of my life. Although you are not here with me to see this accomplishment, I can hear you saying, as you always did, "You can do anything that you put your mind to." I know that you had your own hurts in life but that did not stop you from taking me in and loving me the best way that you knew how. I love and miss you so much.

Larry N. E. King, my father. I know that you would be proud of your '*Boo*'. There is no one that I meet, that knew you, that doesn't say how much I was your pride and joy. I wish that we would have had more time together but I am thankful for the time that God did allow us to have and the closeness that we shared before you were gone. When I smile, I see you. I always said that you could never deny me because I look and act too much like you, lol.

Rose-Marie King, my mother. Without you I would not be here. Although circumstances didn't allow us to be together most of my life, I believe that you cared for me the best that you could. Over the years we have had our challenges and triumphs. You have overcome a lot of trials in your life also. Seeing you continue against all odds helped me to see that it was possible for me too. I love you, ma.

Pastor Kent Barnes, mentor and friend. God put me and my husband on your heart during a time that I had lost all desire for the church. You never pressured us but was loving, understanding and still uncompromising with the Word of God. I thank God for you and I truly believe that you are a pastor with the heart of God. Thank you also to the body of One Nation Kingdom Ministries for welcoming me and my husband as family. I love you all.

Thank you to my friends and family who over the years have beckoned me to write my poetry for others to hear and enjoy. Thank you for encouraging me and believing in me. I thank you for allowing me to share my poems with you over the years and letting me see that they weren't only for me but that they could help, encourage and heal others also.

Introduction

I have written poetry and other literary works in the past for recreation or because of school assignments. I didn't realize how much writing would become a part of my life. I had gotten through a bad marriage just before writing the works of which you'll read in this book. During and following the divorce from my ex-husband came escapades with strange men. I didn't know the person I had become and neither did those who were close to me. Headed down a fast spiral of destruction, I prayed for God to lead me to a church home where I could finally begin my healing process; a place where His Spirit would dwell, a safe place.

God led me to a church in a neighboring city thirty minutes away from the city I lived in. My grandmother had begun dialysis October of 2003 and God assigned one of her nurses to me who was also a minister at the church I had begun attending. After visiting for two weeks I became a member, and my healing process began. I had no idea what was in store for me and my family.

December 2004 my grandmother passed away, the same week that she was buried my father started dialysis. Two months later I was diagnosed with end stage Renal Failure. I was diagnosed with high blood pressure, sleep apnea, and I learned that I not only had one working kidney but it was only functioning at thirty-five percent. Yet, in all these life changing situations, God has been faithful; showing his everlasting love even in these difficult times. My relationship with Him has grown and now I know that I must trust Him in all things. I must share the gift that He has given me to speak words that others feel, as I do, yet may not have the ability to express them as I'm able.

One evening while spending time with the Lord, He began to speak through me on paper also allowing me to release thoughts and feelings of my own. As I wrote I noticed all the words would take on poetic form, they just flowed freely without thought to all the do's and don'ts that's learned in English literary classes. I am sure my high school teachers and college professors would not be proud, but that was not my concern. I was releasing hurt and demons; I was becoming free. The only rule God gave me was to keep it simple. "NO BIG WORDS," He said. The words were mine but also His, God seemed to take over as I would write, and my hand couldn't keep up with the words as they came to my mind.

After years of seeking counseling through family, friends, pastors and professionals; God Himself, was giving me therapy through poems. Then God had me share these proses of feelings and cries for help with friends and ministries. Little did I know that my first step to deliverance would also begin to free others.

As He has for many others and myself, allow God to minister to you in the midst of your life situations, whatever they may be, as you read "*My Life's Poetry*."

My Life's Poetry
My gift of my life and poetry given back to the Lord

I'm sitting here thinking of all the pain in my heart
And all the mess in my head
Not able to decipher my end from my start
Wishing, hoping it would all end

Words are whisking in my mind demanding to be heard
A misplacing of space and time,
A journey only to be made with words

I have all this inside of me trying to get out,
For once I can express myself not giving to criticism or doubt

So I'm grabbing my paper and pen
Writing of my feelings of now and then

Lord it's as if someone is speaking in my ear
Telling me what to say here and how to emphasize there

I'm trying to state my case, expecting only my words to remain
But the Holy Ghost is saying,
"You have a response for my anguish and pain."

As I take dictation of what You speak,
I know this prose is more than a past time,
Because it's got a hold on me

Wait a minute Lord, my hand can't keep up with what You utter
Please slow down Lord, cause if it's possible
I believe you've caused my hand to stutter

Lord I'm feeling liberation enjoying this release;
I believe I'm hearing reconciliation
What do you mean my words are not just for me?

So now through your lead I have to pray,
Lord, what do you have to say?

Because my experiences shaped me to think the worst,
But the words you give me to write, you're saying
I can break the bind of the curse?

With my tongue that's been known to cut like a sword,
I can now bring to life the Living Word?

How do I become a mouth piece for the rejected, abused,
The ill and the weak?
Lord I hear you saying by continuing to 'write' and 'speak'

So Lord are you saying writing poetry is a gift,
Like the gold and frankincense?
Are you saying writing poetry is worth the same as that?

So if I'm understanding, the worth is not in the value
Of a dollar exchange
But rather it's returning the things I can give back to you
That you gave

Because the talent I have when I share with men
Multiplies its value in Heaven like the servant
Who multiplied his five talents to ten

The gift shared gives others hope in you
So the heart being lifted encourages me while glorifying you?

Thank you Lord, cause I didn't see it that way
So now I know it is important that I share what I have to say

With this being said, I cover my words in Your Blood
And Bless You for the ability to write,
I give up my desire to offer my own insight

Lord, I lay my pen, paper and life at your feet
And submit for your glory, MY LIFE'S POETRY!!!

My Life's Poetry

I Wrote My Name
A Time of Realization

That Sunday, God's judgment was sounded at the House of Worship
His tone said enough, His Word cut quick
Thoughts bombarded my mind from fear but I dare not quit

Learning to walk with fear and trembling
Taking account for my own soul
Desiring to get this thing right
Careful to tread wherever I may go

God began to give me practical ideas
To get out of the messes I was in
Encouragement either with a smile or rod of correction
Declaring me to win

To triumph over the small things that could grow and become more
To believe Him to get through the big things as He, one by one,
closed each open door

I signed the time card that I may get paid
The stroke of the pen was fierce, the way, in my hand, it laid

My writing seemed elegant each letter distinctive with its own stroke
A signature of confidence, a sign a yoke had broke

This was more than a signature but a declaration of its own kind
As if God, Himself, was writing through me telling me to declare
what's mine

I knew from that point on, I would not be the same
For this was the day that with heart, mind and spirit,
I wrote My name

My Life's Poetry

Why?
A Question of Worth

I said....

Why did my mother hit me?
Why did my father quit me?

Why did I have to be abused?
Why couldn't I be excused?

Why did they say those things to me?
Why were they so mean to me?

Why do I look the way I do?
Why couldn't I be more like you?

Why do I crave food?
Why do I act so rude?

Why did I have to cry?
Why couldn't I have been the one to die?

Why am I here?
Why doesn't anyone care?

Why isn't my hair long?
Why do I always do what seems wrong?

Why couldn't I be more pretty?
Why do these things have to be?

Why don't I have someone?
Why does my time coming seem so long?

God said....

Because I said so
Because I needed you to grow

Because they were in pain
Because their thinking wasn't sane

Because I know the strength I gave
Because I said no to the grave

Because I wanted you to know me
Because you survived, others can become free

Because I know my plans for you
Because if you faint not, you will receive what's due

Because I love who I created
Because I knew all along you'd make it

Because they couldn't keep you from Me
Because I designed you carefully

Because I need no explanation
Because I see your determination

Because I only let satan get so far
Because I wouldn't allow you to remain scarred

Because I want you to know real love
Because I want you not to seek what is below
But rather what is above

Because I heard my Son cry out for you
Because My Spirit beckoned Me to

Because out of others in your family, you received My call
Because of your obedience, they may be saved from their own fall

Because My plan is without repentance
Because I know My faith in you without hesitance

Because I know what you don't know
And simply said, because I said so!

My Life's Poetry

I Am More Than A Conqueror
Triumph In Christ

I know what it's like to be awakened in the middle of the night
To feel a strong hand whip a belt across my hip
To have someone only magnify my flaws
To be treated as if there was no law
Looking to ones I deemed for my protection
To save me and give me direction
Yet the one that I esteemed to love me
Beat me with words and objects to control me

I know what it's like to cry silently in the middle of the night
Remembering the feeling of an unwanted touch
From the one who momma cared for so much
To be told that it was all my fault
When I didn't understand my own body, feelings or thoughts

I know what it's like to feel rejected in the middle of the night
Wondering why daddy didn't show up today
Wondering the next time he would come my way
Watching his affection being awarded to another
Feeling jealous of the love he had for my own brother

BUT ALSO;

I know what it's like to think in the middle of the night
How God mended a broken heart that was torn apart
How He restored relationship with me and my parents
How he gave us understanding and forgiveness
How my obedience to Christ gave my father a new life

He's no longer here to see me smile or hear my laugh
But he is with Christ without suffering; He's at rest

I know what it's like to realize in the middle of the night
How blessed I am:
I've survived physical and sexual abuse
I've survived rejection and anxiety
I've survived displacement and misunderstanding
I've survived death and loss of loved ones
I've survived sickness and disease

I cry ABBA FATHER and my God delivers me from all my troubles
He is glorified in my suffering and uplifted in my testimony
He is magnified in my joy and honored in my overcoming

I know what it's like to hear God in the middle of the night
To say "Have faith regardless of what it looks like"

I know what it's like to praise God in the middle of the night
BECAUSE I AM MORE THAN A CONQUEROR!

My Life's Poetry

Seeking Love
Looking for love in all the wrong places

Desiring love, seeking sex
Desiring love but not understanding it

Desiring love and falling in love with food
Desiring love but not knowing if love really loves you

Desiring love yet overcome by the shortcomings
Desiring love and yet loving those not deserving

Desiring love and never being satisfied with attention
Desiring love and not being able to keep anyone

Desiring love and needing a gentle touch
Desiring love yet hating self so much

Desiring love and holding everyone else responsible
Desiring love and not understanding they don't know how to

Desiring love, a stranger I heard of and never met
Desiring love and yet it seeks me without rest

Desiring love to come and make Himself known
Desiring love but my desire is running cold

Who is this love and when will He find me
Who is this love that said He would never leave nor forsake me

Did I see Him and pass Him by?
Is He wondering where I went to, while I ask why?

Is he near but I turn away?
Is he still interested after I have laid
With the men, the food, the thoughts, the tunes
The TV, the CDs, the things I wanted and the things of need?

Will He still accept me, the one who committed adultery
The one who said, "Yes I am free" just to be in a deeper valley
emotionally?

How patient shall He be desiring to love the one who runs from Him
The one who has forsaken His righteousness for sin over and over
again

I understand when David desired to be erased
Why Elijah desired to be replaced

Why Job lost site for a moment
When everything around him was destroyed and his body lay sore
and bent

Yet love brought him back to himself, a state beyond restoration
A faith in his beloved that lacked hesitation

Love who came to save a world from itself
Who offers to those who refuse His help

This love, the love I question with my doubt
This love that I render powerless because of the fear within that
leaves me without

This love l-o-v-e
E-el-o-him

L-O-V-E, life of vision eternal
Life that is spoken by written word of the Anointed One

Love not found in sex or chocolate
Love not found in man or woman, father or mother
Love that sticks closer than a brother

I hear in a close distance, I love you
I see in a near future, what I am called to

I pray that this love will break every yoke
I pray that this love will fix what is broke

I pray that this love will not let me go
I pray that this love is the love that I will die to live fo'

Love, l-o-v-e
E-el-o-him

This love that I continue to seek
This love that has found me.....

My Life's Poetry

I Was Looking For God One Day
Where is God so I Thought

I was looking for God one day but I got distracted by a butterfly
I watched it flash its wings of brilliant color then lift off and fly

I was looking for God one day and I got distracted by the rain
As I watched the drops fall almost strategically not one hitting the ground the same

I was looking for God one day and I got distracted by a baby's smile
As I gave her my attention, she blew me a kiss and lovingly, once again smiled

I was looking for God one day, I needed an answer for life
But I got distracted by a man passing by who stopped to ask, "Are you alright?"

I was looking for God one day and got distracted by my pain
Yet a stranger took time to encourage me and said, "Don't worry sweetie this thing shall not remain."

I was looking for God one day and got distracted by what the doctor said
But I heard a voice within saying, "I will resurrect that which is dead."

I was looking for God one day and got distracted by what I lacked
But I felt a push lift me up as if a strong tower upheld my back

I was looking for God one day but got distracted from the memory
of abuse
Yet a woman that remembered me and had been watching my life,
shared my story to her good use

I was looking for God one day but was distracted by my father's
death
Yet in my heart I had peace knowing he had changed over the years
and now his face showed he was at rest

I was looking for God one day and got tired so I stopped
But I heard a voice say my name and I felt my heart drop

Lalea, it's me, I AM that I AM, your God of WHOM you seek
"My God, My God" I said, "I've looked but why did you leave me?"

"I never left", He said, "For I was there with you all along."
"Each time that you sought me I appeared in a different form."

I sent the butterfly of brilliant color for you to see my beauty
And when you were standing in my reign I was responding to your
cry "Lord wash me"

The baby that smiled your way, I had asked to send you my kiss
And the man that showed concern, I sent to let you know your
thoughts were not missed

And the one I sent to encourage you in your pain
I placed in your path that day because she prayed for someone to
bless out of her pain

And when the doctor diagnosed you with the disease of which your
father and grandmother had succumb
I chose you that these generational curses would be broken, in you
my hand will move and my works be done

23

And when I saw you focused on what you did not have
I was the strong tower, which upheld you to keep you on your path

And when you were caught up by the thoughts of perverse acts brought against you as a child
I reminded you of your purpose and strength that caused another one in their suffering to have hope and a reason to smile

And when you lost your father, I knew that you didn't understand
I showed how by your walking in my truth, encouraged him and how before I took him, he became a better man

And just when you decided to give up because you didn't realize all along that you were seeing me
I got your attention and opened your eyes and let you know that any time you seek My Word, My Voice, My Direction, My Love, with you is where I'll always be

I SAW GOD THAT DAY!

My Life's Poetry

A REAL WOMAN
Stopped defining myself by others

I once was told that a real woman has curves
She has cellulite, maybe a wrinkle or two and constant talk of low fat, no carbs gets to her nerves

A real woman may have her hair in a ponytail or flipped to one side
And if she's feelin the mood it may be dyed, fried and laid to the side

A real woman may or may not have a man
She knows the Great I AM
And focuses not on what she can't but rather what she can
….do, that is

A real woman sometimes needs some help
Is not too afraid to say NO
And sometimes GET IT YOURSELF

A real woman is not necessarily a size 2
Who only wears Donna Karen shoes
And is always looking for more weight to lose

Rather she may be a size 8, 16 or 20
May shop at Payless or JC Penny
And looks in the mirror and says who's lovin me sure has plenty

To love, to live, to share, to give

I'm a real woman with character and hips
I have strength in my mind and on my lips

The thoughts I share are to get people thinkin
I'm not a Toyota, and experience with me to like drivin a Lincoln

I'm not bad on the eyes and my words are encouraging to the ear
My wisdom is food for the soul and my worship keeps His Holy Spirit near

Yeah, I may not be in Vogue, don't pose for Elle
But my presence speaks all its own without a word to tell

I'm beautiful, wonderful, created He, me
I'm sensational, remarkable and because of His righteousness, I am made Holy

Many may apply but only a selected few may enter in
But you must add or multiply to my worth, I'm not into division or subtraction

Cuz I'm a real woman, the King's daughter, a princess
Come correct cuz neither my Daddy or me are taking any mess

I don't need your definition to define me
And I don't need your caged concepts; I've been set free

I don't even need you to acknowledge I'm here
Because if you don't love me right, I'm not the one you need to fear

I may not wear a 2 piece when I swim
And I may not fog your glasses to the rim

But maybe that's because you need artificial beauty to define you
Or maybe you can't see what's in front of you clearly because you obstruct your own view

Well you are your own problem, not mine
But I do know, not a better me you will ever find

And to my sisters, black, white, dark, light, short, tall, big or small
No man, no friend can love you like you and God can

God says not to think more highly of yourself then you ought
But to not think highly of the Creator and love the created (meaning you) is against what was taught

Know Him, know you, love Him, love you
You know why?
Because God loves real women too!

My Life's Poetry

If This Cup Would Pass
Dealing with Kidney disease

If this cup would pass, then how joyful I would be
No worrying about protein, potassium or failing kidneys

No more hypertension and drugs
No more sitting waiting for results

No more despaired looks and aahs
No more "but you're still so young"

No more swelling of my legs, feet and joints
No more counting and calculating, what would be the point?

No more wondering if God was disappointed and had given me up
No more back and forward in my mind, "You gotta fight", "No, just give up"

No more comparing myself to others feeling this is so unfair
No more limping from gout as people watch and stare

And if I passed there would just be no more
But wondering will God welcome me with open arms or shut Heaven's door

Yet something deep inside won't let me stop
The voice of God encouraging me not to give up

What if you fight? What if you win?
What if someone you love gains strength because of what you did?

What if all your hopes come to pass?
What if your story can help others to last?

What if your fears were diminished to faith?
What if God moved all Heaven and earth for your sake?

What if you live and give life to a son?
Think about being able to share all the battles his mommy had won

What if you were never in danger at all?
But that God allowed it for you to stand lest you fall

What if your victory was on its way?
But you gave up to your fears and missed the results of your faith

What if you died and left your work undone?
What if another lost their life because you weren't there to teach them how to run

What if you find out that your fight wasn't really about you?
What if God just wanted to show you how much He truly loves you?

That he would draw you to Himself out of your need
That He'd rather allow a little suffering to hold you close instead of you living in comfort and separated from Him

God wasn't afraid of my fits, tears, tantrums, and screams
He didn't turn away because of my anger, fear, idle words and shame

He just simply reminded me not to give up
And that He would always be with me as I endure this cup

My Life's Poetry

I KNOW THE THOUGHTS I HAVE TOWARD YOU
God's thoughts are above my thoughts

For I know the thoughts I think towards you of a good expected end
Thoughts of seeing those things I've called in your life, not things imposed by man

To see my Image in you as you become established and perfected
To direct each step that you make and you personify My Presence

You question your gift and purpose not in remembrance that it is given without regret
So until My Word produces through you, what it was called to do, you won't be dismissed just yet

Who can question the call on your life, and who can speak ill of My Word?
Who can question what I've chosen you to be, that they may blot your name from the book?

Have I not said it once and now yet say it again, that you are called by my election?
Do you run to another to meet your need, give you counsel, or be your protection?

Is it Me you revere in your thoughts when you are tempted?
Do you adhere to My Voice when others have left you rejected?

For what fault do I have if I raise you up or cast you aside?
What cause can you put against Me if I choose to leave or abide?

Yet despite any sin against Me or any idle word spoken
Yet twice before and now a third, I say you are My chosen

It is not by a man's order that you can follow My plan
Not even My prophet will speak to you unless I say he can

It is I who gives you breath and I who may take it away
Choose whom you shall follow, choose ye this day

Incline your ears unto me, set your affections on above
Speak My Truth, be bold, listen to wisdom, speak and do in love

For out of your belly shall flow issues of life
Out of your belly shall flow peace to calm the strife

Out of your belly shall flow direction for change
Out of your belly, you shall witness to others of My name

It's not in title, not in deed
It's not based on merit, but by My Spirit, in Me

You live, move, in Me you have your being
Walk by faith, seeing is not believing

Speak only what I've told you
No other voice should make you to move

What lies have been told to you?
Do you not remember My Truth?

For whatever I have declared unto you is indeed My prophecy
For I've shared what I've already decided to do and you are just getting in agreement with Me

Continue to listen for My instructions for I am speaking in continuous motion
Do not reduce Me to a feeling, a hunch, an unction or a notion

Return to the day of your joy just to commune with Me
Return as a baby who delights when he hears daddy

Return as when your first spiritual steps were taken
And you walked with Me, trusting in Me, when your faith in Me had not yet been shaken

Return in heart as a baby
Although you have spiritually grown as a man
Except that you return as at first new breath
And you did all you could to stand

Then shall you be ready to be deployed to what is next for you to do
Then shall you know and not just believe in Me; I shall abide in you

Then shall your vision be made plain
For the plow, be steadied your hand
For I know the thoughts I think toward you of a good expected end

My Life's Poetry

I LEFT AND TIME WOULD NOT WAIT
Fear, procrastination and being stagnant

I left the present to keep revisiting my past
But the memory of what was overshadowed the hope I had last

Time would not wait to allow me to catch up
Time could not wait for the Maker had timed time just enough
Time had no mercy, no compassion, no love

I left my position, felt tired, needed a break,
But when I returned to myself
My slumber had become my very state

…of mind, of being, of moving, of seeing

Time would not wait to allow me to catch up
Time could not wait for the Maker had timed time just enough
Time had no mercy, no compassion, no love

I thought I could buy time, pay in installments
But then when the call came, some things I had to forfeit
More time, some blessings, a few opportunities but not the testing

Time would not wait to allow me to catch up
Time could not wait for the Maker had timed time just enough
Time had no mercy, no compassion, no love

I finally left the excuses, the fear and the shame
Tired of time running out on me over and over again

Seeing the extension of His arms opened wide
While slowly but surely time keeps passing by

Why wouldn't time, for a moment, just stand still
Why couldn't time, for a second, stop turning on its wheel?

How can something that has no end seem in such lack?
How can something that seems to fast forward never be turned back?

Time will not wait to allow me to catch up
Time cannot wait because God has timed time just enough
Time has no mercy, no compassion, no love

CONTENTS

My Life's Poetry

<u>YOU WERE WORTH IT</u>
I am valuable

Thinking about two men that had become a part of me
Thinking of losing the one in need of the other to be free

Words exchanged, feelings entangled
Limbs interwoven, a heart left mangled

One had the covenant but didn't enjoy the benefit of it
The other with whom the covenant was broken which after my faith
Had been choked

Now alone cause I served the one and got served by the other
No word spoken with the legal one
Yet craving more than words from the other

I had lost myself in a grip so tight
That I had lost all strength to fight

No praying and meaning it
After despising what I thought yesterday how much I needed it

Now the one no longer spoke because the meal ticket was redeemed
And I was now just a convenience for the other
Since he knew how to make me scream

I sit knowing my only intention was to love
But thru a turn of events I no longer recognized who I had become

Yet a still small voice would always seep through the cracks
Pleading, warning, wooing me to turn back

It wasn't either of the two men
I knew this voice but it was different from them

I never felt ashamed when He called my name
I never felt hurt or with him questioned my worth

I would just feel peace
Like something fresh in the room was released

But my cravings would scream back
Putting a pain in my neck

Left once again to fend on my won
Left once again to be all-alone

Yet in the silence and between tears
A comforting voice returned to me as he did thru the years

I asked Him why wasn't I worth fighting for, why did they leave?
I hear His Spirit then say to me

I fought for you;
I've called to you the whole time, to bring you back to me
Of course you are worth it; you've always been worth it to me

My Life's Poetry

A TWINKLE IN HIS EYE
Daddy's lil girl

Thinking of less than I am
Thinking of the greater I could be

Thinking of the prisons in which I've been held
Thinking of what could make me believe I'm free

Remorseful because my heart pangs and my body craves
Guilty of what runs through my mind day after day

Thinking of pleasures I believe I am missing
Being held, made love to and kissing

Wanting arms and a smile to greet me when I come home
Wanting to share laughter and memories with a family of my own

But God doesn't scold me like I think He should
He doesn't try to control me like I think He would

But rather He smiles and holds me and I feel His peace
He embraces and consoles me and I feel relief

I wonder why He smiles when I've done nothing to deserve it
But He says to me
You are worthwhile for Me to encourage you not to quit

Yes, you've gone through a lot that would make many to crumble
But even in your hardness, your inner parts seek to be humble

No, you are not perfect in your eyes but in Mine you are made whole
You can only see what is currently but I see the growth

So cry when you have to and don't be afraid
To come to Me in My Son's name

For although your heart hurts and your body craves
It's Me who you turn to by the end of the day

I know you don't understand and you often ask why
Just know to stand because you are the twinkle in my eye

My Life's Poetry

<u>NO ONE KNOWS</u>
Jesus Knows

No one knows the pain you felt when they mocked your name
No one knows the weight you carried
When compared to others, you weren't the same

No one knows all the tears you shed from rejection of who you are
No one knows the journey you've made from where you started
And how far

No one knows the prayers you sacrificed for others that betrayed you
No one knows the places you've had to find refuge
In knowing what you had to do

No one knows the intensity of the pressures on you in this world
No one knows the capacity you've carried
Or how often you've cast your pearls

No one knows the rejection you felt when you reached out to others
No one knows the suffering you felt when betrayed by one
You considered like a brother

No one knows the fight that you fought to keep your faith
No one knows how many times you wanted to forfeit your race

No one knows the yearning your heart felt
Sometimes when you were alone
No one knows how much under that smile you've given, you groan

No one knows the relationship you have with God
But everyone seemed to have advice to get you out of situations
Of which they had no understanding of

The pain to have to take a stand when all others comply
The strain to make amends of hearts torn from others' lies

And in all this we wonder does Christ really understand
In all this we forsake remembering He too was a man

In all His sufferings for our sake
We make Him to prove His love to us over and over again

Well, I'm here to tell you
If you were to hear these words a second time,
You wouldn't think the same

Because these words I wrote to My Lord Jesus,
Concerning His suffering and you thought it was about you
And substituted your own name

You think no one knows, but oh, He knows!!!

My Life's Poetry

DELETED SCENES
Character is born

We each have a story to tell of our own
From the youngest to the ones full grown

The credits we've given to people undeserving
The proceeds we've given to the wrong people unknowingly

The director wasn't really your mother
And although he helped to produce you,
The producer is not your father

The title, unlike many stories, is still unknown
The ending entails growth of seeds yet sown

The admission is of no cost you can give
The editor foresees the life you shall live

The sponsors supply every need known and unknown
The writer ensures that the full story is told

You have now come to the date of your release
But you still concern yourself if the audience will be pleased

To those who thought they knew your story
You have now become a new creature,
And to those your story will set free,
They will seek your bonus features

Rejoice in your outtakes, for they didn't take you out

Gleam for the director's commentary, for it gives you understanding

Allow the diversity of languages your story shall be interpreted,
For you may touch others nation wide

Some may see you in wide screen for a fuller picture
Others may see you in full screen because they held close with ya

At times God may zoom in on a particular shot
To show others when you fainted not

And every now and then He'll return to the main menu
To direct the viewer on a different venue

However, there is one feature that has yet to be seen
The scenes from which your true character was weaned

They were hidden from viewers you tried to impress
They were the parts of your story that caused you lack of rest

You sometimes wished you could erase them from your story
But then would God truly receive the glory?

Til now you controlled who viewed them, you had the remote control
But God had to expose them in order to save your soul

Now your story lay on the shelf to be seen but not sold
The price of its worth and the cost of its making
Exceeds the value of Gold

He placed you in a plain folder, no thrills on the cover
Just a title marked clearly in big bold letters
... A TRUE STORY

This movie not rated by woman or man
Length of viewing, just long enough for you to understand

Special Edition, best on the shelf
Proof of purchase, a change in thyself

Spirit Surround Sound, Digitally Mastered by the Master
Some violence, some strong language and a lot of laughter

Critics say, a star is born, an enlightenment, a must see
But the most astounding attribute, check out the DELETED SCENES

My Life's Poetry

DON'T TELL ME HOW STRONG I AM
Learning that people mean well many times when they cause hurt

*I've lived thru so much sometimes it amazes me
How others can see a current snapshot and think that they know me*

*I've survived physical and sexual abuse
Being exposed by family, being teased and misused*

*Being torn away from home, not knowing who I am
Even taken advantage of in the church,
Indecently advanced to by a so called godly man*

*Overcame divorce twice without skipping a beat
Because I learned how to survive when all I had was me*

*Even living with an illness that took my father
And both of his parents
Not sure what my destiny or what my journey would end with*

*Going to treatments alone, praying this could be another way
Trying to keep it together and be thankful for my days*

*If I hear one more person tell me how strong I am, I will scream
Because my needs are like everyone else's,
It's just that when I cry there's no one around to hear me*

*I don't want pity, or to be patronized
No oohs and ahs and please no sighs*

45

But just give me your smile and a hug now and then
Be a friendly acquaintance or maybe acquaint yourself as a friend

Because this life is hard and it's easy to feel alone
Don't assume that I'm always OK
Because my smile can be deceiving, you know

I appreciate your time, the calls, and laughs
I appreciate everything that I've had

I just ask this one thing if you don't mind
Don't tell me how strong I am
But offer a little strength to me sometimes

My Life's Poetry

DESTINY
In God's hands

Born for a reason
Born for a season

Born to fight
Born to take flight

Born to die
Born wondering why

I can't stop
Wanting to give up

Hope beyond hope
Barely staying afloat

Blessings along the way
Darkness turning to day

Seeking love, finding hate
Being on time but feeling too late

What's it all for?
Who opened this door?

Feeling the flow of my pen
To heal me over and over again

Hurt after hurt
Pain beyond pain

Suffering loss
To reap gain

Broken hearts
Lives torn apart

Relationship mended
Of the one who sent it

Ignorance was bliss
The innocence is missed

Knowledge adding to sorrow
Seeking purpose in tomorrow

Trying to accept that it is what it is
Trying to understand what is this

A face with a name
A past full of shame

One man and his love
To redeem me to His Father's love

This life continues
In search of destined venues

With hope that never fails
His destiny for me shall prevail

My Life's Poetry

HE GOT ME
Games boys play

A conversation on the phone
A conversation that, for once, didn't leave me feeling alone

His words crystal clear
His words seeming so sincere

I'm here for you
If you need me, call me, boo

Don't guess who you are
I can tell you're different by far

His advice of the men's game
Piercing my mind, my heart, over again

Telling me of the conquest for me
That another man will not let me get free

Because I was different than any he'd had
And to conquer my exterior would make him feel more of a man

I'm a conquest? I thought
A contest? No, I'm not

But the more he spoke
The more I choked

I could hold this one close
I'd learn things about men I'd otherwise not know

But his conversation shortly changed
Am I now his conquest? This is strange

It's as if the devil told me about himself
So that I may trust him so that he could take what was left

Addicted to his voice
Feeling there's no other choice

Expecting the call
To be lifted for another fall

What is still in me that I can't stop?
I feel depleted from bottom to top

Praying to God while my mind races
Saying I don't want to be caught
Yet putting myself out there for the chases

God help, I cried
God help before I die

I see there is more purging to be done
Lord, keep my feet that I won't fear and run

I've calmed down now
Telling God how

The saved man played me hard
And the unsaved man almost got my heart

The high that lasted for 3 weeks
Then finally ended at a dreadful peak

When God brought me back to myself
And said, come-on get up, from me comes your help

The lesson of temperance once again failed
A train not crashed but derailed

And God said, "But don't you see my grace?"
"You didn't last as long as before in this place"

You know the cost of what you wanted to do
You even finally faced your worst enemy, YOU

Now I know that you feel left alone
But I am returning you fully to me, a place unknown

Do not fret because of what you think you see
But know my power is ALL power because when they got you,
They got Me

My Life's Poetry

GOD CHOSE ME Y'ALL
God has a plan for me

Why am I depressed, God You chose me
Why am I so stressed, God You chose me

Why heavy laden, God You chose me
Why am I strainin, God You chose me

Wait a minute, I didn't apply, yet God You chose me
I don't know why, but God You chose me

I didn't pass the test, God You chose me?
I know I'm not the best, God You chose me?

Man this seems too hard, but God You chose me
Are You sure that this is my part? God You chose me

I don't know what to do, God You chose me
You want me to represent You? God You chose me?

Ok, ok, I give! God You chose me
To you my life I give! God You chose me

Just please have mercy and patience, remember God You chose me
And don't forget forgiveness and Your graciousness,
Because God You chose me

You know Lord, I don't know why You chose me
He said, "Because there is NO other that replace
Who I've called you to be!!!

52

My Life's Poetry

GOD ALLOWED US TO WALK SIDE BY SIDE FOR A WHILE
Letting go of my relationship with my best friend

God allowed us to walk side by side for a while
He allowed us to talk and to share our smiles

He gave us moments that were small
But left a big impression through it all

I'd hoped that our time together would always last
But sometimes the future has no room for what was in the past

And my present is a designated meeting of time and a place
Although you're no longer beside me,
What was exchanged cannot be erased

Whether perceived as good or bad
It was something special that we had

A connection by the blood
That's now separated us in spite of

Trying to hold on, not able to let go
Saying 'yes' when in my spirit ran 'NO'

So God had to make the break cut dry and clean
And tho it doesn't seem so now
He did it cause He loves us, not because He's mean

So in faith, I trust we are both where we need to be
God has not forgotten you and He's not forgotten me

And every now and then He allows me to remember you and I smile
Because God let us walk side by side for a little while

My Life's Poetry

MY FIRST REAL DANCE
I danced with an Angel

It was in a room full of people
A building made for a steeple

The sounds, the songs, the cries
The people with wonder in their eyes

I felt him call me
His desire for me

I looked to my left
I knew his arms would give me rest

Come be with me
Come commune with me

With tears falling
I stopped stalling

And walked over to him
It wasn't the touch of man but of a true friend

He asked me to dance
How could I lose this chance?

To be embraced by this one
To be embraced by the Son

As I loved him in my heart
I knew that this was a start

Of an intimacy
Never known to me

Not prudish but proper
I could hear him say to fear, don't stop her

Come to me and feel my touch
The feeling you've desired for so long and so much

I felt his arms outstretched and hold me
My body felt lite and my soul was at ease

His cheek touched mine so soft and so sweet
I felt only air between the floor and my feet

He held me so close as if to say, "I'm here"
"I'll never leave you, so don't you fear"

He held me as long as I needed
He took my inhibition for closeness and freed it

He was so kind
For this moment, he was mine

He ushered me into a Holy presence
Compared to others' touch I wouldn't resent this

He held me as to never let go
We danced while he held me close

I could hear the others in the room
But my heart, only he could move

I saw him as handsome with a strong stature
Built as a fortress to protect me from forces of nature

He wasn't of this world, yet very real
Eyes could not behold his profile, but his touch I could feel

As my body prepared to return to itself
And the consciousness of the physical world it had left

I felt him let go, but not as to say goodbye
But rather, I'll meet you here next week, same time

I don't know his name or his address
But he is wonderful, and beautifully arrayed with Heaven's best

He was my Angel sent to me from God
More than a dream and definitely not a mere facade

We've seen each other time and time again
And our beginnings are always matchless to our meetings' ends

But I'll never forget when he gave me that chance
To know what it's like to have my first real dance...

CONTENTS

My Life's Poetry

THINKING OF THE LOVE HE HAS SHOWN ME
Appreciating me through God's eyes

He is pleased when He sees me smile
He's tickled when He hears me laugh
He's the first to compliment my style
Encouraging me to not hold back

He holds me in my time of sorrow
And never complains of my tears
He doesn't hold me to what may come tomorrow
And doesn't count against me the hurts of yester years

He is always willing to take me wherever I may need to go
He responds to my 'yes' but is never deterred by my 'no'

He is my protector at all times
Morning, noon or night
I am precious and cherished in His eyes
Never to be left out of His sight

He never complains that I talk too much
And doesn't get bent out of shape when I tell Him I need His touch

I can talk to Him about anything
He never seems to mind
I can share any need
And He has never been less than kind

He just gets me
Who am I kidding? He's got me and I am His too

It's an understanding, that's it, no need for labels like;
Shawty, baby or boo

And did I tell you how we share time that is only for us
A time that we like to call pillow talk

A time when He will open His thoughts to me
A time when He sees fit to share all His affections for me

It's not a lust thing, it's a love thing, it's mature
Not focusing on just one's need but focusing
On each other's, it's beautiful, it's pure

It's a knowing of His want for me and me for Him
It's a pining that in each other's heart we both may live

Just for me He would move all Heaven and Earth
Because to Him, I have priceless worth

He is my best friend, confidant, the Lover of my soul
By Him my heart has been caught
He is the only one that has made me forget
The others that did not make the cut

When He whispers, I love you; it penetrates my very being
That tears swell in my eyes to the point they stop me from seeing

And it's in that moment that every hurt, every pain
I've ever felt melts away because His love for me
Over powers the dislikes of others and makes every doubt fade

But there is this one thing, He did, that to this day
I just cannot stop thanking Him for
It compares to no Hallmark card, dinner
Or surprise being delivered at my door

It is the most selfless gift one has ever given me
That money cannot buy
It is the most heartfelt gift that makes me ask Him, why?

It is the most astonishing act of love anyone has ever shown for me,
The comparison is none
It's when He sacrificed, for me, His Only Begotten Son

Now that's Love!

My Life's Poetry

WHY HAVE FAITH; WHERE DOES THAT LEAVE ME?
A question of my faith

Faith is the substance of things hoped for and the evidence
Of what is not seen
And if it is impossible to please God without it
And I lack it, then where does that leave me?

If I would ask anything in Christ's name and believe that it will be?
Yet He does not give what I requested
Then where does that leave me?

I spoke to my mountain, told it to move and to be cast into the sea
But the mountain appeared to stand firm
So where does that leave me?

My Father, Abraham, has been noted for his faith
Holding fast to a promise, which due to disobedience, he did not see
Although, God is no respecter of persons
If Abraham's faith did not get him to the Promised Land
Then where does that leave me?

God, why give us faith, when you have the last say so
When you have the final plea?
If I say that I trust in your Word
Yet don't trust the path you've chosen
Then where does that leave me?

Hope deferred is rottenness to my bones
Yet hope is the only air I have to breathe
If my hope of hope seems desolate, then where does that leave me?

God answered...

If I am the Alpha and Omega, knowing all things to be
Yet, you continually do the opposite of what I tell you to
Then where does that leave me?

If delighting yourself in me gives joy and peace is found in me
Yet knowing this, you continue to seek refuge in man or things
Then where does that leave me?

I gave you promises and they still stand
I told you I would keep you from no good thing
But you despise what I love
Holding yourself back from the One Above
Then where does that leave me?

I know the heart you have; I know the pain you live
I know your desire to be free
But I want you to have trust and open yourself
Do you understand where that would leave me?

My hand would direct and bless your path
Open your spirit to innumerable possibilities
Allow forgiveness and understanding
Embrace correction and change, and you'll have wisdom and power
Then you would know where this leads me

Into the hearts of many, who like you, have questioned 'why me'?
And would gain the faith to believe, then that would lead me

Into the lives of the hopeless, the helpless, the fatherless
The ones feeling abandoned and rejected
All things by which you have been set free
And would become the hope, the help
And the bridge in the gap between man and me

Sharing your words of hurt, of love, of failure, of success
Of times you've enjoyed in your life and of times you've bereaved
But when the story is told, you and others, would better understand,
THIS is where God wanted me to be

So I thought....

From the victim to victor, faithless to faith**ful**
From that which once held me captive

Now directed me in my journey of freedom with Elohim
Joy filling my heart, once bound by hurt, now marvels
At the result of having faith and gives praise to God
Because of where this faith has led me

My Life's Poetry

CAUGHT UP

Others hurts acted out towards me as a child started me on an unhealthy journey

Momma introduced me to life: she said she loved me
But I became her whipping bag
A scapegoat for those who hurt her in their authority

I got caught up

Daddy had no daddy to love him and teach him how to be a man
So when he fell short with me, his worst to him was his best
And he said "Boo, I did all I can"

I got caught up

Grandma didn't have affection
Or many kind words to nurture her life
So she hid in silence, in liquor and in becoming a stranger's wife

Her and her husband hadn't learned trust
Yet being together within only three months of introduction
Seemed to be a must

She had her one-way ticket off of an island of pain
For him a beautiful woman he would gain

Yet, his insecurities as an orphan turned into lust
And because of an unquenched desire, came an unwelcomed touch

I got caught up

Relationship after relationship trying to cover the pain
Thinking, I know that this time I'll do better, I won't mess up again

Not understanding that a man couldn't give me joy
Not knowing that my heart was crying out for more

More than what he could say or what he could do
Constantly thinking, I'm not the one with the problem
It's always you

Changing partners in friendships, trying to find somewhere to fit in
Wondering when is my life and my happiness gonna begin

The more I'd try, the more I'd seem to fail
How can I get off this track? How can this train derail?

My head spinning thinking I gained more understanding
Yet the more confused I'd be
And the more I searched and tried to change Lalea, the less I felt me

A vicious cycle that I didn't even start
But because of my perpetuating actions,
I had become very much a part

I got caught up

In someone's depression, another's stress
And someone's self deception
Now I'm finding myself as an addict
Having loneliness and befriending rejection

I got caught up

In a person's twisted mind
And finding the reasons that I would do these things
Were of another's influence, the desire wasn't even mine

I got caught up

But one day after many tears, many fears and a very broken heart
Someone introduced me to this Jesus
Who said my ending would not be as my start

Now at first I didn't understand and sometimes just got plain mad
Yet something on the inside of me knew that this thing
I now possessed was so much better than what I once had

A time to stand and a call to reality
Although another's actions were responsible for my pain
I must hold my reactions into accountability

All those people now had a different perspective and place in my life
My future no longer stood on whose daughter I was,
Whose granddaughter or whose wife

Now don't get me wrong, I love these people
That's why what they did hurt so much
But now this Jesus was showing me real love

See what I was committing was idolatry
Because I didn't have Christ, although He had me

My heart was set on my family's thoughts of me
I was trusting in others who were bound, so how could I be free?

But Jesus, yet mocked and scorned
Was not bound as man, and for this purpose He was born

To set captives free and give abundant life
He only could restore my soul
And illuminate the dark places in my life

Now finding myself in a deliverance process,
Sometimes kickin and cryin
Yet rejoicing on the inside
Because my spirit is no longer dyin

Now my soul and flesh are no longer in control as before
By demons that had entered my life through others' opened doors

But rather God is now closing and has closed doors
Which can never be opened again
Not by situations, not by circumstances and definitely not by man

And what doors God opens can never be shut
And I'm thankful today to say that in Him

I've got caught up

My Life's Poetry

TEMPTATION
Wanting to be wanted

Temptation called and I said Hi
Not totally surrendering but not ready to say bye

Knowing what I was feeling wasn't real
Knowing this was the enemy using him to steal

My job, my praise, the balance of my days
My hope, my love, my focus on Him above

Temptation made me smile, made me feel wanted
Temptation appeared and continually in my thoughts haunted

My view, my perception
I felt wanted, not rejection

But I vowed to Christ my time
Now he was brought to anger because I was His, no longer mine

I told temptation to come clean today
I can't say I even prayed

But I did tell God I didn't want the façade
Of something more that felt real when all had been real odd

I knew what would come next
The lack of sleep and in sleep no rest

The false love and relationship that could form
That would leave me hurt and bruised
While temptation would return to a life of norm

Temptation thought it was fun
I wanted to know temptations intentions,
I wanted to know where all this came from

But I was growing tired of temptation's charm
I knew in the end temptation would only bring me harm

So today I told temptation to come clean
I wasn't rude, condescending or mean

But temptation came to me with a soft violence
And I had to take on temptation with direct force
I had to recognize its true source

So I'm sure temptation won't feel like having me now
Because today I called temptation out

God keep me that I may be kept
Teach me that my desires won't let

Me pull from thee to welcome temptation back
Today I told temptation to come clean and temptation left

My Life's Poetry

I CHOSE TO BELIEVE HIS LIES
No one wants me

I chose to believe his lies
I was sure why I did
Wanting so bad for him to feel
All the things he said

Always wondering what's wrong with me
Why he won't stay
Beating myself up for what, only God knows
Asking God for things I know I shouldn't have prayed

Desires seeming to torture my soul
Wanting to sooth my pain
Craving for someone to hold me
Someone whose heart I'd gain

Not just arms to grab my waist
And lips to kiss mine
But to truly be held
And be taken from time

Needy, sometimes, but who isn't
Wanting, sometimes, my heart felt imprisoned

Is he out there, one who will see my princess cut?
How my brilliance shines?
Under the coal that appears on the surface
Due to my emotional mines

Will he see that I've climbed over great obstacles in my life
To get to where I am now
Will he get in the ring and fight for me
Or walk by and throw in the towel?

I chose to believe your lies because I wanted to believe you
You lied to me thinking I wouldn't learn the truth

But you knew when I walked away without turning back again
That something was now different in my heart
Compared to back then

I'm not mad at you, I just finally believe in me
I decided to go with truth, and truth has set me free

So I say good bye, not as an enemy, nor as a friend
I simply choose to press on and to never believe the lies again

My Life's Poetry

HIS WILL
Submitting what I want for myself for what God wants for me

I had my life planned, or so it seemed
I knew where I wanted to be and when, I thought I knew this thing

I'd escape my troubles by making up my own world
Rethinking the way I was made, desiring lighter skin
And longer hair with curls

Wishing I could be someone else's daughter,
Someone else's child
Then maybe my life would have been normal,
Then maybe I could smile

I used to dream days away and imagine through the night
Escaping reality in my mind was the only way I knew how to fight

See, then I didn't have to feel pain or know any hurt
I sought something that made sense, something pure and clean
But my mind was soiled and my body felt like dirt

Made unclean by another's touch
And unworthy by another's words
Why would such an unimportant life
Be turned over to this world by birth?

Low self-esteem, huh, if that's what you want to call it
Knowing who I really was in others' eyes is how I saw it

See this was life for me
Some people have it hard and some are just plain lucky

Some people are meant to be happy and some people just are
Some people have it easy and some people have it just that hard

Yeah, I was at a place to accept that this was my life
Didn't dream of being a mother, didn't want to be a wife

Didn't know where life would take me
Waiting for the one last thing to break me

Wanting to look in the mirror
And see a different reflection
Wanting to know I was important enough
For someone to be my protection

The names, the games, the cruel things said
Many days and nights left me wishing I were dead

But I thought this was how it was supposed to be
If not meant for others, for some reason meant for me

Then as the years crept through
God would slowly reveal the lies which had become my truth

I won't lie;
It seems sometimes more painful to heal than to hurt
But the opportunity to love life and help another cannot repay
Deliverance's true worth

I went through it all for a reason
And now God has graced me to this season

To laugh and to cry
To ask and learn why

To share without shame
To glorify His Holy Name

To comfort and to forgive
To love and to live

To know and to understand
And to see all my CAN'T's with Him, I CAN

Through abuse and abandon
Through beatings and blame
Through mental anguish
Through heartache and pain
Through betrayal and divorce
Through loves found and loves lost
Through depression and being alone
Through longing for things unknown

I'm still here I made it through
Thank you, Lord, I couldn't be here if not for you

I still have questions, which I am sure you know
And with time you'll continue to reveal as I continue to grow

This journey is not done and there is much more to go through
Thanks again, Lord, because I can't do it without you

My Life's Poetry

HELP ME LORD; A SPIRIT'S CRY

We buried Grandma just weeks before I wrote this poem. She was mom to me
having raised me. I really needed God to make it day by day

My mom had to let me go
Because she couldn't cope

My father wouldn't show his face
Because he couldn't stand in his place

My grandmother loved me
The best way that she could
But her husband violated my innocence
And told me that I misunderstood

Now grandma is gone and there is nothing I can say
But now that she has gone, contentment has moved on its way

I don't know what grandma was trying to hide
But when she left this world, she said more than goodbye

Her death has allowed new life, new beginnings
I feel like her losses have become my winnings

Skeletons falling out of the closet
All I can think is, Lord, what's next?

How do you handle, knowing you were never wanted?
How do you deal with a past estranged and haunted?

The pain, sometimes I feel and sometimes I'm numb
This time of my life seems dark with an eclipse of the Son

Lord, I said I won't turn away, you are all I have
But my days, although filled with laughter, end with me feeling sad

Please Lord; allow me to still reach out,
Please continue to show me how to love
I pray for your peace to rest on me
Just as the fig tree gave rest to the dove

My life does matter, why else would you have given it form?
It's just my search for fulfillment and meaning is so torn

The tears, they fall yet have nowhere to land
The hurt comes out, yet it feels it will have no end

Lord, I need you now, I think more than ever before
I don't know if I can continue to put on the smiles anymore

My friends, they try to help with their words
But the majority of the time, I leave feeling more hurt

How do you explain what you don't understand?
And how do you continue to walk this path
When you don't even feel like you can stand?

I know you love me; I choose to believe you do
But sometimes I feel so confused
I can't or should I say, don't turn to you

I know that even in my pain, I must remember to stay humble
Lord, I ask just to be able to see some light at the end of this tunnel

Thanks for keeping me although I don't feel kept
And thank you for rest
Even though I can't remember when I actually slept

I know one day you may reveal this plan that I live, this plan surreal

But until then Lord, please allow peace
And Lord, I pray your mercy

I know I've fallen away from some things that I know
Yet part of me believes you're allowing it for me to grow

Please pull me back Lord, I can't lose you too
If I did Lord, what could I possibly do?

To know your Word and not perform it is sin within itself
But I feel like some things have just been stored on the shelf

Until when? Till I'm better, till the grief is gone?
Till I'm bitter? Till your mercy is worn?

I pray not, please don't let me go
I plead that you would know

I don't want to turn away, with you is where I wanna stay

Lord please keep me, Lord please free me

From my pain, from my past, from circumstances that didn't last
From people, from myself, from false aides I turned to for help

I need you Lord: I need you now
With broken heart and contrite spirit, I bow

From the depths of my soul and the spirit of my mind
From the joy in my talents, and the pain that encourages me to write

HELP ME LORD!!!

My Life's Poetry

HE LOVES ME

A dedication to my father, Larry Noel Eugene King. God used this poem to bridge the gap between us before taking you home. I love you and miss you daddy!

I didn't understand as a little girl why when I called your name,
You weren't there
I misunderstood because of your actions
And thought that you didn't care

I didn't understand why you never reacted
When I'd share my heart with you
I misunderstood that you had your own pain and didn't know what
To say or do

I didn't understand how another woman
Could get more of your time then I did
I misunderstood that you were able, with her, to keep things well hid

I didn't understand why sometimes you would get so angry
Over what seemed to be small things
I misunderstood that no one could know what was in your heart
And things your mind would think

I know you hurt and you can't let the world know
But don't let anger and resentment continue to grow

You have so much love to give; I've seen it in your eyes
And although I've only viewed it twice in my life
In my heart, I've heard your cries

I used to think that you were using money to buy my affection
And at first, I will admit that it did get my attention

But over the years, through the pain and in my walk with God
I know now that your offering me your substance
Is a way of offering yourself
Letting me know you care and showing me love

I thank God for you all though we've had our share of arguments
But I'm focusing on now and the future
Not what happened way back then

I do love you daddy and I know you love me
I pray that you would open your heart more and not fear being free

It is a risk to let others in and, yes, sometimes it hurts
But every once and a while God will bless you with others
That will show you true friendship and what true love is worth

You are special to me and to God
Look to God to see what He can still do in your life,
Don't look at what you did not

This message I send to you with love and true affection
Things people have said and the way you were treated
Is not your true reflection

God created your life with purpose
I wouldn't say that if I didn't know that it was true
He created you because
He has a plan that no one else can fulfill but you

In the days to come, don't wonder what could have been in the past
But rather allow God into your heart
So that He may show you what He has for you ahead

81

God gave me this poem especially for you
And He wants to tell you how much He loves you too

Say a prayer tonight and for Him to increase your faith
Repent of all your sins and receive Him in your heart today

He's waiting to hold you and to show you things you never dreamed
He really loves you daddy
And I'm glad He chose your daughter to be ME!!

My Life's Poetry

Her Eyes
Grandma says "So long till we meet again"

She can't speak, well at least not at most times
But her eyes tell a story so true, but ones that have been covered
with lies

What I once thought was, I know now could not be
But her eyes say it all, they tell the whole story

Her strength is like none to be compared
Her compassion knew no end

Her patience was worth noting
Her contributions to all around her were noticed by others' doting

Like I said, she can't speak
But her eyes say, "Lea, I'm weak"

"Honey, grandma loves you" I could hear her say
"But grandma's tired, with the Father is where I'll be I pray"

"You know what's right and always look up to the Father"
"Only He know what's best, He'll watch over you"

"Be sure to zip your coat to keep your chest from the cold"
"If you don't, you'll feel it in your joints when you get old"

"Lock your car doors and be safe"
"You shouldn't be out that late anyway"

"I've had you with me most of your life"
"I've watched you grow from baby, to lady, to woman and a wife"

"I'm proud of you and what you did in school"
"Remember not to let your left hand know what your right hand is
doing. Be cool"

"Don't cry over me when I leave from here"
"Just remember all the good times we shared"

"Remember everything that the Father has brought you through"
"And to your own self, be true"

"Read your Bible and continue to pray"
"And we will be seeing each other again one day"

"Now sweetheart, grandma's tired, please let me go
"Home to the Father and always know"

"Don't carry hate in your heart, the Father sees all"
"When you feel down, on the Father you should call"

"The others who hurt me, don't be angry with them"
"I've finally found the one who sticks closer than a brother,
A true friend"

"Thank you for your prayers and thoughts"
"I told you when the Father was ready for me, He'd let me know"

"Now go on with your life and what God has for you"
"I've seen some of the wonderful things He's placed in you to do"

"Now honey, I'm tired, grandma's getting ready to go and rest"
"Tell Pop and Daddy, I love them and give them my best"

"Father only knows what this life may bring"
"But don't worry about me no more; I'm going home
 To rest with Him"

"You know I don't like goodbye
Makes me feel like something will go wrong"
So her eyes looked at me weak and tired and said, as she would have
"So long"

On the following page you will find a song that the Lord gave me some years ago. I was asleep and I had dreamed of a church choir singing this song. I even heard a woman singing the lead so clear. When I woke up, I immediately grabbed a pad and pen to write down the lyrics. I couldn't get this song out of my head.

As I meditated on it throughout the coming days of that week, the Lord showed me how this song is filled with words that could be in the heart of a person seeking a deeper relationship with the Lord or someone coming into the knowledge of Christ. I pray that these words bless all who read them.

It's Not Too Late

(It's not too late)
It's not too late to say thank you Jesus
(It's not too late)
It's not too late to tell You how I feel
(It's not too late)
It's not too late to repent and turn to Jesus
As long as you have breath, it's not too late

If you would like to receive Christ as your personal Savior and Lord, or would like to rededicate your life to Christ, please say the following prayer.

Dear Lord Jesus, I repent of my sins and ask that you would come into my heart. I thank you for your sacrifice for the forgiveness of my sins and reconciliation to God, the Father. I believe that you are the Son of the living God and receive your love and salvation this day. In Jesus Name, Amen.

You do not have to walk this journey alone. Please pray for God to guide you to a Word of God teaching church with a Pastor that has his heart. If possible, purchase a King James Bible, a concordance and a dictionary. I believe God to guide you and teach you in His Word through His Holy Spirit and that your life will never be the same.

Me and Memories of Daddy, Grandma and My Brother… R.I.H.
Gone but never forgotten!!!

www.ingramcontent.com/pod-product-compliance
Lightning Source LLC
Chambersburg PA
CBHW062020040426
42447CB00010B/2088